What's a mammal?

There are more than 4,000 different kinds of mammals. All mammals are vertebrates. This means they have backbones. They also have these things in common.

Mammals are warm blooded. The temperature inside their bodies stays about the same whatever the weather.

polar bear

cat feeding kittens

Mammals look after their young and feed them on milk from the mother's body.

koala

Mammals
have some hair
on their bodies.

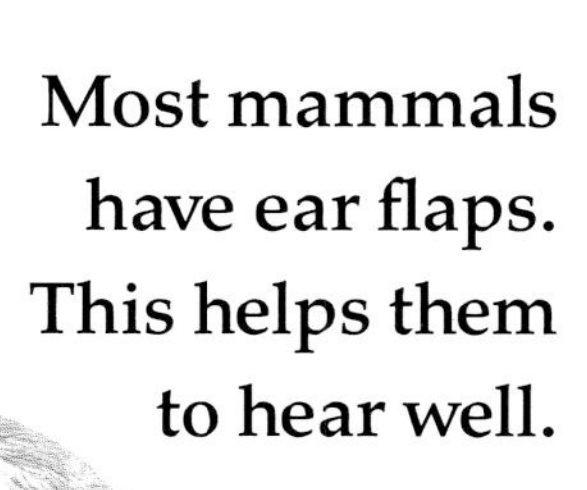

Most mammals
have ear flaps.
This helps them
to hear well.

All mammals have lungs.
They breathe air to stay alive.

hare

Who's who?

Mammals are all sorts of different shapes and sizes. Can you match these shapes with the animals opposite?

hippopotamus
gorilla
bat
lioness
rat
raccoon
armadillo
elephant

Covered with hair

Hair helps to keep animals warm. It traps air and keeps out cold, wind and rain.

yaks

Mammals that live in cold places have very long hair.

Some mammals have hardly any hair at all.

Indian elephant

llama

panda

Fur, wool, prickly spines, smooth scales and even some horns are all made from hair.

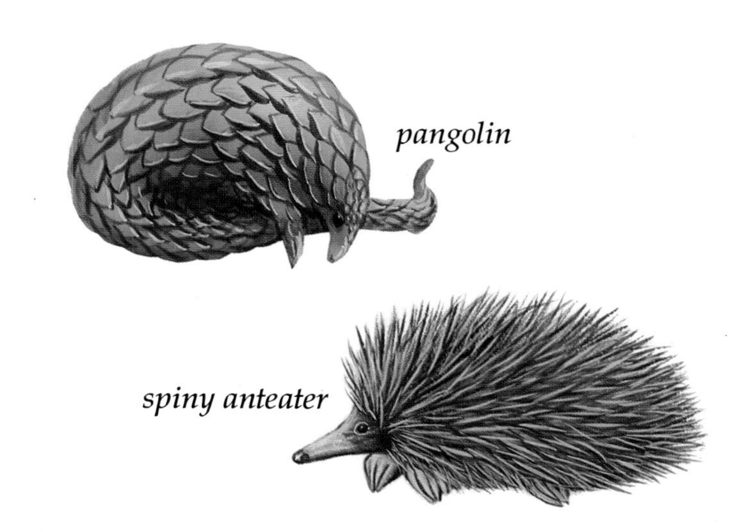
pangolin

spiny anteater

What's what?

Which mammal:

- provides us with wool?
- has spines to protect itself?
- has a horn made of hair?
- lives in a very cold place?

Open the flap to find out.

Clever coats

The colour of a mammal's coat may help it to hide from its enemy or to stalk its prey. This is called camouflage.

Can you find these animals hiding in this picture?

striped linsang

leopard

tiger
sloth
baby tapir

Eyes, ears and noses

Most mammals can see, hear and smell very well. They have eyes, ears and noses to suit the ways they live and feed.

proboscis monkey

A male proboscis monkey honks loudly with its nose to warn of danger.

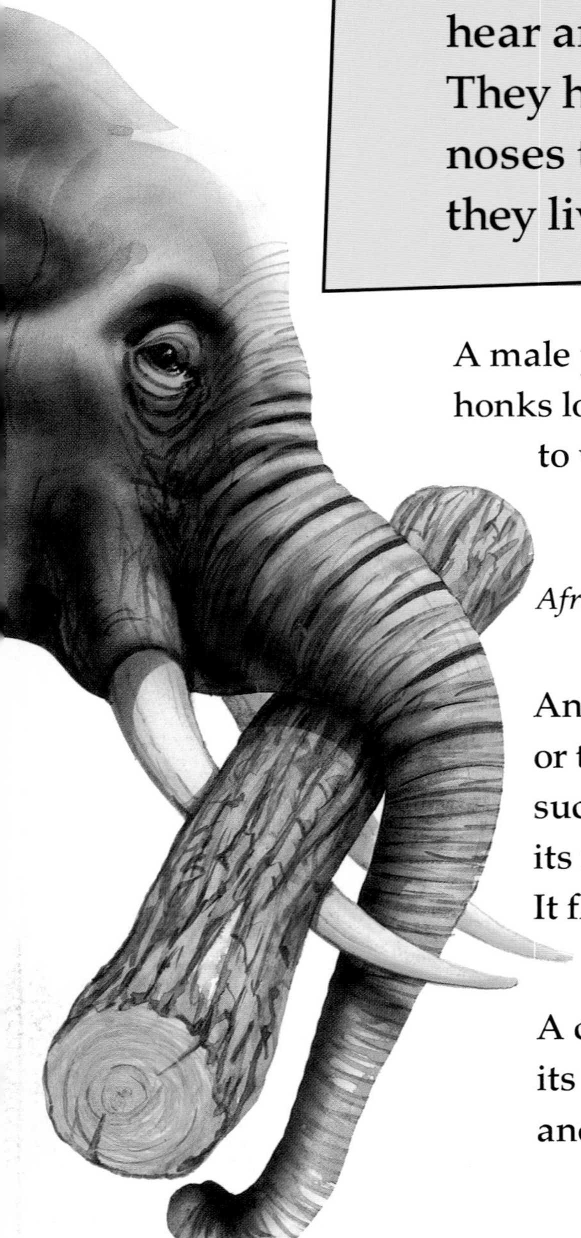

African elephant

An elephant uses its long nose, or trunk, for picking up food, sucking up water to squirt into its mouth and for lifting things. It flaps its ears to keep cool.

A camel can close its nostrils to stop sand and dust getting in.

Arabian camel

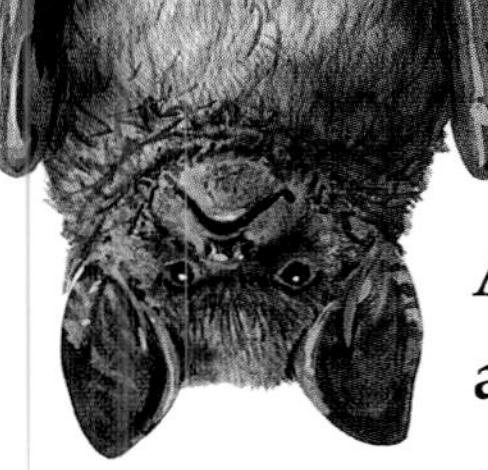

brown bat

A bat can hear better than any other land mammal.

bushbaby

A Jack rabbit's big, long ears help to keep it cool in the hot desert.

Bushbabies can pick up the sound of tiny insects moving at night. Their big eyes help them to see in the dark.

Jack rabbit

Many hunting animals have eyes facing forwards. This helps them to judge how far away their prey is before they leap on it.

wolf

On the move

All mammals move about to find food and to escape from danger.

gazelle

Animals with long, slim legs can move swiftly across the ground to flee from their enemies.

hippopotamus

Big, strong animals often have short, sturdy legs.

prairie dog

Burrowing mammals often have strong front legs for digging holes or burrows.

kangaroo rat

Animals with big, strong back legs can jump high and leap across the ground.

What's what?

Which legs are good for:

- supporting a big mammal?
- jumping?
- burrowing?
- running?

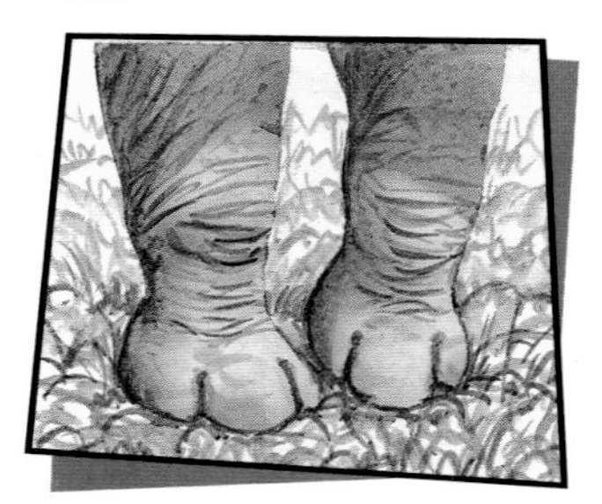

Open the flap to find out.

Home, sweet home

Mammals make their homes under the ground, up in the treetops and in caves. Some live in the water, others just wander from place to place.

Animals that live in herds do not make a home. The babies are able to walk soon after they are born, so they can follow the herd.

Harvest mice build tiny nests on grass stems.

Beavers build homes, called lodges, in the water. They make them out of logs, twigs and branches.

Rabbits and moles live under the ground in tunnels or burrows.

In the winter, some bears dig dens or find caves to live in.

At night, orang-utans make beds from branches and twigs in the fork of a tree.

Bats sleep in dark caves, hollow trees and empty buildings or hang from the branches of trees.

Big eaters

Mammals need to eat lots of food to give them energy. Different mammals eat different kinds of food.

Animals that mostly eat plants are called herbivores. They have flat teeth to grind up the leaves.

red deer

tamandua

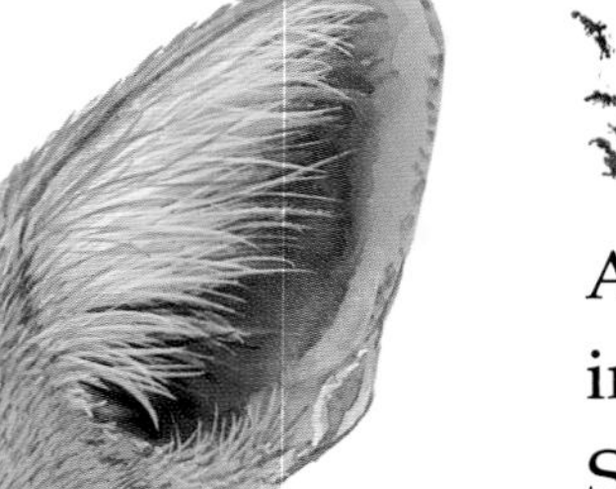

Animals that eat ants and other insects are called insectivores. Some have long, thin tongues.

jackal

Animals that mostly eat meat are called carnivores. They have sharp fangs to stab their prey and to slice up meat.

chipmunk

Rodents have big, sharp front teeth which keep growing. They eat nuts, seeds and grains.

Omnivores eat all kinds of food, including meat, fruit and plants. Some even eat fish and honey.

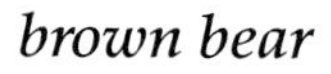

brown bear

What's what?

Who eats what?

giraffe

lion

giant anteater

squirrel

Open the flap to find out.

Baby mammals

Mammal mothers look after their babies and feed them until they are old enough to find their own food.

Baby hunting dogs start eating meat when they are two weeks old. Their mother coughs up food she has swallowed to feed them.

A Virginian opposum may have as many as 15 babies at once. When they get too big to fit in her pouch, she carries them on her back and tummy.

A lioness teaches her cubs everything they need to know. They learn how to stalk and pounce on their prey.

Baby baboons love to play. They chase each other about and pretend to have fights.

What's what?

Can you match the babies with their mothers?

Open the flap to find out.

Record holders

dolphin

The highest jumper

A dolphin can leap up to 20 metres out of the water.

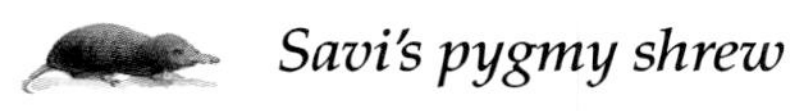
Savi's pygmy shrew

The smallest mammal

A Savi's pygmy shrew is about as big as your thumb.

male giraffe

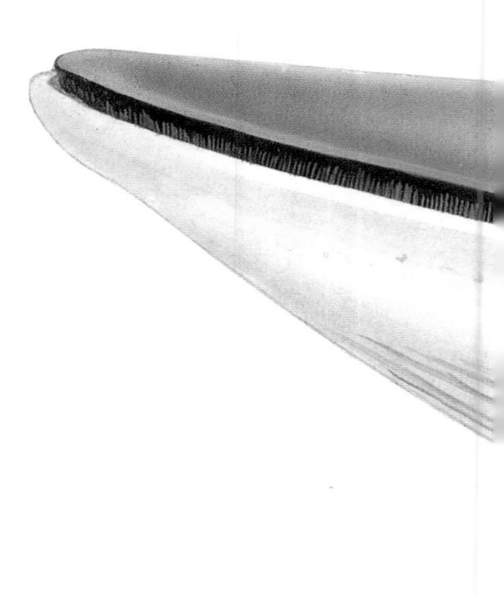

The tallest mammal (by far)

A male giraffe is taller than two men standing on top of each other.

The slowest mammal

A three-toed sloth moves across the ground at only two metres a minute.

three-toed sloth

The fastest runner

cheetah

A cheetah can run up to 110 km/h over a short distance.

The biggest mammal of all

female blue whale

A female blue whale is about 100 million times heavier than the tiny pygmy shrew.

Mammal quiz

What can you remember? Look back through the book to help you find the answers.

giraffe

musk ox

1. Is a giraffe a carnivore, herbivore or omnivore?

rabbit

3. Does a musk ox live in a hot or cold place?

2. Where does a rabbit makes its home?

4. Does an elephant use its ears to keep cool?

African elephant

5. Whose legs are these?

lion

jackal

mountain goat

6. Which mammal is the odd one out?

hyena

7. Which of these is a mammal?

crocodile

toucan

tiger moth

human

Open the flap to find out.